My AI Agent: Ultimate Beginner's Guide to Building an AI Agent with Python

Master AI automation step by step using free frameworks and tools

Chapter 1: Introduction to AI Agents

What is an AI Agent?

An **AI agent** is a software program that perceives its environment, processes information, and takes actions to achieve a specific goal. AI agents range from simple rule-based systems to advanced machine-learning-driven models capable of decision-making and automation. They are commonly used in applications like customer service chatbots, task automation, data processing, and even autonomous robots.

Key Characteristics of AI Agents:

- **Autonomy:** Operate without constant human intervention.

- **Reactivity:** Respond to inputs and changes in the environment.
- **Proactivity:** Can initiate actions to achieve goals.
- **Adaptability:** Learn from data and improve over time.

How AI Agents Work: Inputs, Processing, and Actions

AI agents function through a structured process involving three main components:

1. **Perception (Input Handling):**
   o Collect data from various sources (e.g., text, images, speech, sensors).
   o Utilize APIs, databases, or direct user interactions.
2. **Processing (Decision-Making):**
   o Use predefined rules, machine learning models, or neural networks.
   o Process and analyze data to determine the best course of action.
3. **Action (Output Generation):**
   o Generate responses (e.g., chatbot messages, automated emails, task execution).
   o Trigger automated workflows or interact with other systems.

Real-World Applications of AI Agents

AI agents are widely used across various industries. Here are some practical examples:

- **Customer Support:** AI-powered chatbots and virtual assistants handle inquiries, troubleshoot problems, and provide 24/7 assistance.
- **Data Processing & Analysis:** AI agents automate data entry, extract insights from large datasets, and assist in decision-making.
- **Task Automation:** AI-driven scripts automate repetitive tasks like scheduling, email management, and workflow execution.
- **Finance & Trading:** AI bots analyze market trends and execute trades based on pre-set conditions.
- **Healthcare:** AI assistants help with medical diagnosis, patient management, and personalized treatment recommendations.

Overview of Free & Open-Source AI Tools

To build AI agents efficiently, developers often use **free and open-source tools**. Here are some popular options:

- **Python:** The primary programming language for AI development due to its vast ecosystem.
- **OpenAI API Alternatives:** Free models like GPT4All, DeepSeek, and Mistral for language processing.
- **LangChain:** A powerful framework for building AI-driven applications.
- **Auto-GPT & BabyAGI:** Open-source AI agent frameworks that automate tasks.
- **TensorFlow & PyTorch:** Machine learning frameworks for training AI models.
- **NLTK & spaCy:** Libraries for natural language processing (NLP).

What You Will Learn in This Guide

This book will take you through a step-by-step journey to **build your own AI agent** using Python and free tools. You will:

- Learn the **fundamentals of AI agents** and how they work.
- Set up your **AI development environment** with free frameworks.
- Build and deploy a **fully functional AI agent** for practical use.
- Explore **real-world applications** and optimization techniques.

By the end of this guide, you will have hands-on experience creating an **AI-powered automation system** that can handle tasks efficiently. Let's dive in!

Chapter 2: Setting Up Your Development Environment

Installing Python and Jupyter Notebook

To begin developing your AI agent, you first need to install Python and Jupyter Notebook, which will allow you to write and test your code efficiently.

Step 1: Install Python

1. Download the latest version of Python from the official website: https://www.python.org/downloads/.
2. During installation, ensure the **"Add Python to PATH"** option is selected.
3. Verify installation by opening a terminal or command prompt and running:
4. ```
   python --version
   ```

   or

   ```
   python3 --version
   ```

Step 2: Install Jupyter Notebook

Jupyter Notebook provides an interactive coding environment, useful for testing AI models and visualizing results.

1. Open a terminal or command prompt.
2. Install Jupyter Notebook using pip:
   ```

```
3. pip install notebook
```
4. Start Jupyter Notebook by running:
```
5. jupyter notebook
```

This will open a browser window with the Jupyter interface.

Essential Python Libraries for AI Development

Once Python is installed, you'll need key libraries to work with AI models efficiently. Install the following essential packages:

```
pip install openai langchain transformers gradio
requests numpy pandas matplotlib
```

Library Overview

- **openai** – Access OpenAI's GPT models.
- **langchain** – Build AI-driven applications with structured prompts.
- **transformers** – Leverage pre-trained AI models.
- **gradio** – Create simple web UIs for AI applications.
- **numpy & pandas** – Data processing and manipulation.
- **matplotlib** – Data visualization.

Setting Up API Keys

To use AI services from OpenAI, Hugging Face, or Google, you'll need API keys. Follow these steps to set them up:

OpenAI API Key

1. Sign up at https://openai.com.
2. Go to **API Keys** in your account settings.
3. Generate a new API key and store it securely.

Hugging Face API Key

1. Sign up at https://huggingface.co.
2. Navigate to **Settings > Access Tokens**.
3. Generate a new key and keep it safe.

Google API Key (for AI and Cloud Services)

1. Visit Google Cloud Console.
2. Create a new project and enable the relevant AI APIs.
3. Navigate to **Credentials** and generate an API key.

To use API keys in your scripts, store them in environment variables:

```
export OPENAI_API_KEY='your_api_key_here'
export HUGGINGFACE_API_KEY='your_api_key_here'
export GOOGLE_API_KEY='your_api_key_here'
```

Or, in Python:

```
import os
os.environ["OPENAI_API_KEY"] =
"your_api_key_here"
```

Creating a Virtual Environment for AI Projects

A virtual environment isolates your AI projects to avoid dependency conflicts.

Step 1: Create a Virtual Environment

```
python -m venv ai_env
```

Step 2: Activate the Virtual Environment

- On Windows:
- `ai_env\Scripts\activate`
- On macOS/Linux:
- `source ai_env/bin/activate`

Step 3: Install Required Libraries in the Virtual Environment

```
pip install -r requirements.txt
```

(You can create a `requirements.txt` file containing all necessary libraries.)

Step 4: Deactivate the Virtual Environment

When you're done working, deactivate the environment by running:

```
deactivate
```

Conclusion

By following these steps, you've successfully set up your AI development environment, installed essential tools, and configured API keys. You're now ready to build and experiment with AI models!

Chapter 3: Understanding NLP and Large Language Models (LLMs)

Introduction

Natural Language Processing (NLP) and Large Language Models (LLMs) are the foundation of modern AI-driven text generation and chatbot applications. Understanding how these technologies work will help you effectively develop and deploy AI agents. This chapter covers key concepts such as tokenization, model training, and the differences between fine-tuning and prompt engineering.

How Large Language Models Work

LLMs are a subset of artificial intelligence trained to understand and generate human-like text. They rely on deep learning architectures, specifically transformers, which process vast amounts of textual data to learn patterns, syntax, and context. The core components of an LLM include:

- **Training Data**: LLMs require large datasets of text from books, websites, and other sources.
- **Neural Networks**: Transformer-based architectures (e.g., GPT, BERT) use self-attention mechanisms to analyze relationships between words and generate coherent responses.
- **Tokens**: Text is broken down into smaller units (words, subwords, or characters) to help the model process language efficiently.

- **Inference**: When given a prompt, the model predicts the most probable sequence of words based on its training data.

Free & Open-Source LLMs

Several open-source LLMs are available, providing flexibility and cost-effective alternatives to proprietary AI models. Here are some notable ones:

- **DeepSeek**: A powerful, open-source LLM optimized for efficiency and multilingual capabilities.
- **Falcon**: Developed by the Technology Innovation Institute, Falcon offers high performance and accessibility.
- **Llama**: Meta's Llama models are widely used for AI research and development, known for their balance of efficiency and power.

Using open-source LLMs allows developers to modify and fine-tune models according to specific needs without relying on expensive cloud-based APIs.

Tokenization and Text Processing in NLP

Tokenization is the process of breaking text into smaller components (tokens) that a model can understand. There are different types of tokenization methods:

- **Word-based Tokenization**: Splits text into words (e.g., "AI is amazing" → ["AI", "is", "amazing"]).

- **Subword Tokenization**: Breaks words into smaller parts for better handling of rare words (e.g., "unhappiness" → ["un", "happiness"].
- **Character-based Tokenization**: Treats each character as a token, useful for languages without spaces between words.

Tokenization ensures that models process text efficiently while maintaining linguistic meaning.

Fine-Tuning vs. Prompt Engineering

There are two primary ways to customize LLM outputs:

- **Fine-Tuning**: Modifying an existing model by training it on domain-specific data. This requires computational resources but enhances accuracy for specialized tasks.
- **Prompt Engineering**: Crafting optimized input prompts to guide the model's output without modifying its parameters. This is a cost-effective way to improve performance without additional training.

When to Use Fine-Tuning vs. Prompt Engineering

Approach	Pros	Cons
Fine-Tuning	Higher accuracy for specific tasks	Requires large datasets and computing power
Prompt Engineering	Quick and cost-effective	Less control over model behavior

Conclusion

Understanding NLP and LLMs is crucial for building AI applications. Whether using open-source models, optimizing tokenization, or selecting between fine-tuning and prompt engineering, these concepts will help you develop efficient AI solutions. In the next chapter, we will explore practical implementation methods to bring your AI agent to life.

Chapter 4: Building Your First AI Agent (Step-by-Step)

In this chapter, we'll walk through the process of building a basic AI agent using Python. By the end of this guide, you'll have a functional chatbot that can hold conversations, remember previous interactions, and even run locally without requiring cloud-based AI services.

4.1 Creating a Basic AI Agent with OpenAI API

To get started, we'll use OpenAI's API to create a simple chatbot. You'll need an API key from OpenAI and a Python environment with the openai package installed.

Step 1: Install the required libraries

```bash
pip install openai
```

Step 2: Write a simple script to interact with the OpenAI API

```python
import openai

api_key = "your_openai_api_key"

def chat_with_ai(prompt):
    response = openai.ChatCompletion.create(
        model="gpt-4",
        messages=[{"role": "user", "content":
prompt}],
        api_key=api_key
    )
```

```
    return
response["choices"][0]["message"]["content"]

user_input = input("You: ")
print("AI:", chat_with_ai(user_input))
```

This script allows you to send messages to OpenAI's GPT-4 and receive responses.

4.2 Implementing a Simple Chatbot Using LangChain

LangChain simplifies the process of building AI applications by managing prompts, memory, and logic flow.

Step 1: Install LangChain

bash

```
pip install langchain openai
```

Step 2: Create a chatbot using LangChain

python

```
from langchain.chat_models import ChatOpenAI
from langchain.schema import HumanMessage

llm = ChatOpenAI(model_name="gpt-4",
openai_api_key="your_api_key")

def chat_with_langchain(user_input):
    response =
llm([HumanMessage(content=user_input)])
    return response.content

user_input = input("You: ")
print("AI:", chat_with_langchain(user_input))
```

4.3 Adding Memory and Context Awareness

A chatbot that remembers past interactions provides a more natural and engaging experience. LangChain offers built-in memory management.

Step 1: Install necessary packages

```bash
pip install langchain openai
```

Step 2: Implement conversational memory

```python
from langchain.memory import
ConversationBufferMemory
from langchain.chains import ConversationChain
from langchain.chat_models import ChatOpenAI

memory = ConversationBufferMemory()
chat = ConversationChain(
    llm=ChatOpenAI(model_name="gpt-4",
openai_api_key="your_api_key"),
    memory=memory
)

while True:
    user_input = input("You: ")
    if user_input.lower() == "exit":
        break
    response = chat.run(user_input)
    print("AI:", response)
```

Now, the chatbot remembers previous interactions and builds context dynamically.

4.4 Running Your AI Agent Locally

Instead of relying on OpenAI's API, you can run an AI model locally using tools like LlamaIndex and DeepSeek.

Step 1: Install dependencies

```bash
bash

pip install llama-cpp-python deepseek
```

Step 2: Load and run a local model

```python
python

from llama_cpp import Llama

llm =
Llama(model_path="path/to/your/model.gguf")

def chat_with_local_ai(prompt):
    response = llm(prompt, max_tokens=200)
    return response["choices"][0]["text"]

user_input = input("You: ")
print("AI:", chat_with_local_ai(user_input))
```

By running your AI model locally, you ensure privacy and eliminate API costs.

Chapter 5: Expanding Your AI Agent's Capabilities

Now that you've built a basic AI agent, it's time to enhance its capabilities. In this chapter, you'll learn how to connect your AI to the internet, automate tasks, add voice input and text-to-speech, and integrate with messaging platforms like Discord, Telegram, and Slack.

5.1 Connecting to the Internet (Web Scraping & API Calls)

AI agents can retrieve real-time data by using web scraping and API calls.

Web Scraping with BeautifulSoup

Install the required package:

```bash
pip install beautifulsoup4 requests
```

Example: Scraping the latest news headlines:

```python
import requests
from bs4 import BeautifulSoup

def get_news():
    url = "https://news.ycombinator.com/"
    response = requests.get(url)
```

```
    soup = BeautifulSoup(response.text,
"html.parser")

    headlines = [a.text for a in
soup.find_all("a", class_="titlelink")][:5]
    return "\n".join(headlines)

print(get_news())
```

Making API Calls

Example: Fetching weather data from OpenWeatherMap:

```
python

import requests

API_KEY = "your_api_key"
CITY = "New York"

def get_weather():
    url =
f"http://api.openweathermap.org/data/2.5/weather
?q={CITY}&appid={API_KEY}&units=metric"
    response = requests.get(url)
    data = response.json()
    return f"Weather in {CITY}:
{data['weather'][0]['description']},
{data['main']['temp']}°C"

print(get_weather())
```

5.2 Automating Tasks (Email, File Management, Data Analysis)

Your AI agent can perform common automation tasks like sending emails, managing files, and analyzing data.

Sending Emails with SMTP

Install the package:

```bash
pip install smtplib
```

Example: Sending an automated email:

```python
import smtplib

def send_email(recipient, subject, body):
    sender = "your_email@gmail.com"
    password = "your_password"

    message = f"Subject: {subject}\n\n{body}"

    with smtplib.SMTP_SSL("smtp.gmail.com", 465) as server:
        server.login(sender, password)
        server.sendmail(sender, recipient, message)

send_email("recipient@example.com", "Hello from AI", "This is an automated email.")
```

Managing Files

Example: Automatically renaming all .txt files in a folder:

```python
import os

def rename_files():
    folder = "path/to/your/folder"
    for index, filename in enumerate(os.listdir(folder)):
```

```
if filename.endswith(".txt"):
    os.rename(os.path.join(folder,
filename), os.path.join(folder,
f"file_{index}.txt"))

rename_files()
```

Simple Data Analysis with Pandas

Install Pandas:

```bash
pip install pandas
```

Example: Analyzing CSV data:

```python
import pandas as pd

df = pd.read_csv("data.csv")
print(df.describe())   # Show summary statistics
```

5.3 Voice Input & Text-to-Speech Features

Adding voice input and speech synthesis makes your AI assistant more interactive.

Speech Recognition for Voice Commands

Install the package:

```bash
pip install speechrecognition pyaudio
```

Example:

```python
import speech_recognition as sr

recognizer = sr.Recognizer()

def listen():
    with sr.Microphone() as source:
        print("Listening...")
        audio = recognizer.listen(source)

    try:
        return recognizer.recognize_google(audio)
    except sr.UnknownValueError:
        return "Sorry, I couldn't understand that."
    except sr.RequestError:
        return "API unavailable."

print("You said:", listen())
```

Text-to-Speech with pyttsx3

Install the package:

```bash
pip install pyttsx3
```

Example:

```python
import pyttsx3

engine = pyttsx3.init()
engine.say("Hello! I am your AI assistant.")
engine.runAndWait()
```

5.4 Integrating AI with Discord, Telegram, or Slack

Connecting your AI to chat platforms allows for real-time interactions.

Integrating with Discord

Install the library:

bash

```
pip install discord
```

Example bot:

python

```
import discord

TOKEN = "your_discord_bot_token"

client = discord.Client()

@client.event
async def on_ready():
    print(f"Logged in as {client.user}")

@client.event
async def on_message(message):
    if message.author == client.user:
        return

    if message.content.startswith("!hello"):
        await message.channel.send("Hello! I am
your AI assistant.")

client.run(TOKEN)
```

Integrating with Telegram

Install the library:

```bash
pip install python-telegram-bot
```

Example bot:

```python
from telegram import Update
from telegram.ext import Updater,
CommandHandler, CallbackContext

TOKEN = "your_telegram_bot_token"

def start(update: Update, context:
CallbackContext):
    update.message.reply_text("Hello! I'm your
AI assistant.")

updater = Updater(TOKEN)
updater.dispatcher.add_handler(CommandHandler("s
tart", start))

updater.start_polling()
updater.idle()
```

Conclusion:
✅ Connecting to the internet for real-time data retrieval
✅ Automating tasks like sending emails and managing files
✅ Adding voice recognition and text-to-speech
✅ Integrating with messaging platforms like Discord and Telegram

Chapter 6: Deploying Your AI Agent

Now that you've built and expanded your AI agent, it's time to deploy it for real-world use. In this chapter, we'll explore different deployment options, from running your AI locally to hosting it on cloud services.

6.1 Running Your AI Agent on a Local Server

Deploying locally ensures privacy and full control over your AI agent.

Using Flask for Local Deployment

Flask is a lightweight web framework for running AI models on a local server.

Step 1: Install Flask

```bash
pip install flask
```

Step 2: Create a Flask server

```python
from flask import Flask, request, jsonify
import openai

app = Flask(__name__)

api_key = "your_openai_api_key"
```

```python
@app.route("/chat", methods=["POST"])
def chat():
    data = request.get_json()
    user_input = data.get("message")

    response = openai.ChatCompletion.create(
        model="gpt-4",
        messages=[{"role": "user", "content":
user_input}],
        api_key=api_key
    )

    return jsonify({"response":
response["choices"][0]["message"]["content"]})

if __name__ == "__main__":
    app.run(debug=True)
```

Step 3: Test the API

Run the Flask server:

bash

```bash
python app.py
```

Then send a POST request using a tool like Postman or curl:

bash

```bash
curl -X POST http://127.0.0.1:5000/chat -H
"Content-Type: application/json" -d '{"message":
"Hello AI"}'
```

Now your AI agent runs as a local API!

6.2 Deploying AI Using Google Colab or Hugging Face Spaces

If you prefer cloud deployment, **Google Colab** and **Hugging Face Spaces** offer free, easy-to-use solutions.

Google Colab Deployment

1. Upload your Python script to Google Colab.
2. Install dependencies inside a Colab notebook:

```python
!pip install openai flask
```

3. Run the Flask app in Colab:

```python
!python app.py
```

4. Use **ngrok** to expose the local server publicly:

```python
!pip install pyngrok
from pyngrok import ngrok
ngrok_tunnel = ngrok.connect(5000)
print("Public URL:",
ngrok_tunnel.public_url)
```

Now your AI agent is accessible via the internet!

Hosting on Hugging Face Spaces

Hugging Face Spaces allows you to deploy AI apps with minimal effort.

1. Create a new Space at Hugging Face Spaces.
2. Upload your Python script.
3. Add a `requirements.txt` file:

```
nginx

openai
flask
```

4. Use **Gradio** (explained next) or Flask to serve the model.

6.3 Turning Your AI Agent into a Web App with Gradio or Streamlit

You can create an interactive web app for your AI assistant using **Gradio** or **Streamlit**.

Gradio Web Interface

Gradio makes it simple to create an interactive AI chatbot.

Step 1: Install Gradio

```bash
pip install gradio
```

Step 2: Create a simple chatbot app

```python
import gradio as gr
import openai

def chat(user_input):
```

```
    response = openai.ChatCompletion.create(
        model="gpt-4",
        messages=[{"role": "user", "content":
user_input}],
        api_key="your_openai_api_key"
    )
    return
response["choices"][0]["message"]["content"]

gr.Interface(fn=chat, inputs="text",
outputs="text").launch()
```

Running the App

```bash
bash
```

```
python app.py
```

Your chatbot now runs as a web app with a user-friendly interface!

Streamlit Web Interface

Streamlit is another excellent tool for building AI-powered apps.

Step 1: Install Streamlit

```bash
bash
```

```
pip install streamlit
```

Step 2: Create a Streamlit chatbot app

```python
python
```

```python
import streamlit as st
import openai
```

```
st.title("AI Chatbot")

def chat(user_input):
    response = openai.ChatCompletion.create(
        model="gpt-4",
        messages=[{"role": "user", "content":
user_input}],
        api_key="your_openai_api_key"
    )
    return
response["choices"][0]["message"]["content"]

user_input = st.text_input("You: ")
if st.button("Send"):
    response = chat(user_input)
    st.write("AI:", response)
```

Running the App

```bash
streamlit run app.py
```

Now you have a fully functional chatbot web app!

6.4 Scaling and Optimizing Performance

If you plan to scale your AI agent, consider these optimizations:

✓ Using FastAPI for Faster Performance
Replace Flask with FastAPI for improved speed. Install FastAPI:

```bash
pip install fastapi uvicorn
```

Example:

```python
from fastapi import FastAPI
import openai

app = FastAPI()

@app.post("/chat")
async def chat(user_input: str):
    response = openai.ChatCompletion.create(
        model="gpt-4",
        messages=[{"role": "user", "content":
user_input}],
        api_key="your_openai_api_key"
    )
    return {"response":
response["choices"][0]["message"]["content"]}
```

Run with:

```bash
uvicorn app:app --host 0.0.0.0 --port 8000
```

✅ Caching with Redis
Use Redis to store AI responses and reduce API calls:

```bash
pip install redis
```

Example:

```python
import redis

cache = redis.Redis(host='localhost', port=6379,
db=0)
```

```
def chat_with_cache(user_input):
    if cache.exists(user_input):
        return cache.get(user_input).decode()

    response = chat(user_input)
    cache.set(user_input, response)
    return response
```

✅ **Deploying on AWS or Google Cloud**
For production use, deploy on cloud platforms like **AWS Lambda, Google Cloud Run**, or **Azure Functions.**

Conclusion

This chapter covered multiple ways to deploy your AI agent:
✅ Running locally with Flask or FastAPI
✅ Hosting in the cloud using Google Colab or Hugging Face
✅ Creating interactive web apps with Gradio or Streamlit
✅ Optimizing performance with caching and cloud deployment

Chapter 7: Optimizing, Debugging & Best Practices

Now that your AI agent is deployed, it's time to fine-tune its performance, debug common issues, and adopt best practices for responsible AI development. This chapter will cover **prompt engineering, debugging errors, ethical considerations**, and **future trends** in AI.

7.1 Improving Response Accuracy with Prompt Engineering

Prompt engineering is the art of crafting better inputs to get more relevant AI responses. Here are key techniques to improve your AI's accuracy:

1. Using System Messages for Better Control

Instead of an open-ended prompt, provide clear instructions:

```python
messages = [
    {"role": "system", "content": "You are a
helpful assistant that answers concisely."},
    {"role": "user", "content": "Explain quantum
computing in simple terms."}
]
```

Why? System messages set behavior, tone, and response style.

2. Providing Examples for Few-Shot Learning

```python
python

messages = [
    {"role": "system", "content": "You are an AI
that formats responses in bullet points."},
    {"role": "user", "content": "Summarize the
benefits of meditation."},
    {"role": "assistant", "content": "- Reduces
stress\n- Improves focus\n- Enhances emotional
well-being"}
]
```

Why? Few-shot learning helps the model mimic the format you want.

3. Using Role Play for Contextual Accuracy

```python
python

messages = [
    {"role": "system", "content": "You are a
doctor providing professional medical advice."},
    {"role": "user", "content": "What are the
symptoms of vitamin D deficiency?"}
]
```

Why? Role-based prompts improve response reliability for specific domains.

7.2 Debugging Common Errors in AI Agents

AI models may encounter various issues. Here's how to troubleshoot them:

1. Handling API Errors

If your AI agent suddenly stops working, check API rate limits and errors:

```python
import openai

try:
    response = openai.ChatCompletion.create(
        model="gpt-4",
        messages=[{"role": "user", "content": "Tell me a joke"}]
    )
except openai.error.RateLimitError:
    print("API rate limit exceeded. Try again later.")
except openai.error.OpenAIError as e:
    print(f"An error occurred: {e}")
```

Fix: Catch specific errors like `RateLimitError`, `TimeoutError`, and `InvalidRequestError`.

2. Dealing with Hallucinations (AI Making Up Facts)

AI sometimes generates incorrect or misleading information.
Solution:

- Ask the AI to **cite sources**:

  ```python
  "Please include reputable sources in your answer."
  ```

- Use **retrieval-augmented generation (RAG)** to connect AI with real-time data.
- Fine-tune responses with **fact-checking algorithms**.

3. Fixing Slow Response Times

AI responses might lag due to:
✅ **Inefficient API calls** → Use streaming responses.
✅ **Large model size** → Switch to a smaller model (e.g., GPT-3.5 instead of GPT-4).
✅ **High latency** → Deploy AI on **edge computing** or optimize queries.

7.3 Ethical Considerations & Bias in AI

As AI adoption grows, ethical concerns become critical.

1. Reducing Bias in AI Responses

AI can inherit biases from training data.
Solution:
✅ Use **diverse datasets** when fine-tuning.
✅ Apply **content moderation filters** to prevent harmful outputs.
✅ Allow **user feedback loops** to improve AI fairness.

2. Ensuring User Privacy & Data Security

If your AI agent handles personal data, follow these best practices:
✅ **Avoid storing sensitive user input** unless necessary.
✅ Use **encryption** for storing and transmitting data.
✅ Follow **GDPR & AI ethics guidelines** for legal compliance.

3. Avoiding AI Over-Reliance

AI should **augment**, not **replace**, human decision-making.
✓ Clearly state AI limitations.
✓ Always provide a **human review option** where necessary.

7.4 Future Trends & Next Steps for AI Developers

AI technology is evolving rapidly. Here's what's next:

1. Multimodal AI (Text, Image, Audio, Video)

Future AI agents will process and generate text, images, and audio seamlessly.
Example: GPT-4 Turbo can handle **both text and images** in a single query.

2. AI Agents with Memory & Personalization

AI models will **remember previous interactions** and adapt responses dynamically.
Example: OpenAI's **memory-enabled chatbots** for long-term conversations.

3. Decentralized AI & Edge Computing

Instead of cloud-based models, **on-device AI** will become more common.
Example: Running **LLMs locally** using **DeepSeek** or **LM Studio** for privacy-focused AI.

4. Open-Source AI Development

With tools like **LangChain** and **Hugging Face Transformers**, open-source AI will drive new innovations.

7.5 Optimizing AI with DeepSeek

DeepSeek is an **open-source AI model** designed for efficient **local and offline AI processing**. It's a powerful alternative to cloud-based AI models like OpenAI's GPT, offering **privacy, speed, and customization**.

Why Use DeepSeek?

✅ **Runs Locally** – No need for API calls or internet connectivity.
✅ **Optimized for Efficiency** – Lower hardware requirements compared to other LLMs.
✅ **Supports Fine-Tuning** – Customize the model with **your own data**.

7.5.1 Installing and Running DeepSeek Locally

Step 1: Install Required Dependencies

Ensure you have **Python 3.8+** and install `transformers` and `torch`:

```bash
pip install transformers torch
```

Step 2: Load DeepSeek Model

```python
from transformers import AutoModelForCausalLM,
AutoTokenizer
```

37

```
model_name = "deepseek-ai/deepseek-llm-7b"   #
Choose the right model size
tokenizer =
AutoTokenizer.from_pretrained(model_name)
model =
AutoModelForCausalLM.from_pretrained(model_name)
```

Step 3: Generate Responses with DeepSeek

```python
python
```

```python
def chat_with_deepseek(prompt):
    inputs = tokenizer(prompt,
return_tensors="pt")
    outputs = model.generate(**inputs,
max_length=200)
    return tokenizer.decode(outputs[0],
skip_special_tokens=True)

response = chat_with_deepseek("What is quantum
computing?")
print(response)
```

Now, DeepSeek runs **entirely on your local machine**, offering **faster** and **more private** AI interactions.

7.5.2 Fine-Tuning DeepSeek with Custom Data

DeepSeek allows **fine-tuning** for specialized AI applications.

1. Prepare Your Dataset (JSON Format)

```json
json
```

```json
[
  {"instruction": "Explain Newton's laws",
"response": "Newton's laws describe motion..."},
```

38

```
{"instruction": "Summarize AI ethics",
"response": "AI ethics focuses on bias,
fairness..."}
]
```

2. Use LoRA (Low-Rank Adaptation) for Efficient Training

```bash
pip install peft
python
```

```
from peft import LoraConfig, get_peft_model

lora_config = LoraConfig(task_type="CAUSAL_LM",
r=8, lora_alpha=32, lora_dropout=0.1)
model = get_peft_model(model, lora_config)
```

3. Train the Model

```python
trainer = Trainer(model=model,
train_dataset=custom_dataset,
args=training_args)
trainer.train()
```

Fine-tuning DeepSeek allows you to create a **domain-specific AI agent** tailored to **your own needs**.

7.5.3 Comparing DeepSeek vs. OpenAI GPT

Feature	DeepSeek (Local)	OpenAI GPT (Cloud)
Privacy	✓ 100% Local	✗ Requires Internet

Speed	✅ Fast (No API delays)	⚠️☐ Network Dependent
Customization	✅ Full control	⚠️☐ Limited (API-based)
Cost	✅ Free (once installed)	✖ Pay per API request

If you **need full control over your AI agent, DeepSeek** is a great alternative to cloud-based solutions.

This chapter covered essential best practices for AI developers:
✅ Improving response accuracy with **prompt engineering**
✅ Debugging **API errors, hallucinations, and slow response times**
✅ Addressing **AI ethics, bias, and privacy concerns**
✅ Exploring **future AI trends like multimodal AI and decentralized models**
✅ **Prompt engineering** for accuracy
✅ **Debugging AI errors**
✅ **Ethical AI practices**
✅ **Future AI trends**
✅ **Deploying DeepSeek for local AI agents**

Conclusion

Optimizing and troubleshooting your AI agent is crucial for ensuring **accuracy, efficiency, and reliability**. In this chapter, we explored key strategies, including:

✅ **Prompt engineering** – Crafting better instructions for improved AI responses.
✅ **Debugging AI errors** – Handling API issues, hallucinations, and slow response times.
✅ **Ethical considerations** – Reducing bias, ensuring privacy, and promoting responsible AI usage.
✅ **Future AI trends** – Exploring multimodal AI, memory-enhanced agents, and decentralized models.
✅ **DeepSeek for local AI** – Running AI **offline** for better **privacy, cost-efficiency, and customization.**

By applying these best practices, you can build an AI agent that is **more accurate, reliable, and aligned with ethical standards.**

Table of Contents